BY EAVAN BOLAND

An Origin Like Water: Collected Poems 1967–1987
In a Time of Violence: Poems
The Lost Land: Poems
Object Lessons: The Life of the Woman and the Poet in Our Time
Outside History: Selected Poems 1980–1990
Against Love Poetry: Poems
The Making of a Poem: A Norton Anthology of Poetic Forms
(editor, with Mark Strand)

Outside
History

OUTSIDE HISTORY

selected poems
1980 — 1990

by EAVAN
BOLAND

W·W· NORTON & COMPANY

NEW YORK · LONDON

First published as a Norton paperback 1991; reissued 2001

Printed in the United States of America.

The text of this book is composed in Bernhard Modern and Univers #57
Condensed, with the display set in Carson Condensed.
Composition and Manufacturing by The Maple-Vail Book Manufacturing Group.
Book design by Antonina Krass.

Library of Congress Cataloging-in-Publication Data
Boland, Eavan.
Outside history : selected poems, 1980–1990 / Eavan Boland.
p.   cm.
I. Title.
PR6052.O35098   1990
821'.914—dc20   90-31754

ISBN 0-393-30822-7

W. W. Norton & Company, Inc., 500 Fifth Avenue, New York, N.Y. 10110
www.wwnorton.com

W. W. Norton & Company, Ltd., Castle House,
75/76 Wells Street, London W1T 3QT

1 2 3 4 5 6 7 8 9 0

ACKNOWLEDGMENTS

Thanks to the editors of the following publications where these poems, sometimes in different form, first appeared:

The Atlantic Monthly: "The Achill Woman"; "The Latin Lesson"; *The Yale Review:* "The Shadow Doll"; *Ploughshares:* "The Rooms of Other Women Poets"; *Antaeus:* "On the Gift of *The Birds of America* by John James Audubon"; *Pequod:* "The Photograph on My Father's Desk"

The New Yorker: "The Black Lace Fan My Mother Gave Me"; "Mountain Time"; "Spring at the Edge of the Sonnet"; "White Hawthorn in the West of Ireland"; "The River"; "What We Lost"; "Our Origins Are in the Sea"; "Nights of Childhood"; "Midnight Flowers"; "Distances"

The sequence *Outside History* appeared in *PN Review* and *The American Poetry Review.*

"The Achill Woman" and "Spring at the Edge of the Sonnet" appeared in the Poetry Book Society Selections for 1988 and 1989.

"What Love Intended" (as "The Past") appeared in *Soho Square* (Bloomsbury 1988). "The Black Lace Fan My Mother Gave Me" appeared in *Last and Always* (Faber 1988).

The Seneca Review and *Northwest Review* featured poems from *The Journey;* poems from it also appeared in *The Yale Review; The Ontario Review; The Partisan Review; The Agni Review; The Massachusetts Review; The Chicago Review;* and *The American Poetry Review.*

The Journey (the title poem) appeared in limited edition in a Deerfield/Gallery publication.

The Journey and *Night Feed* appeared in another form with Carcanet Press.

Thanks also to: *The Irish Times; The Sunday Tribune; The New Nation; Gown; The Sunday Times; Poetry Review; Poetry Ireland; Oxford Poetry; Orbis.* BBC 2 (television); BBC 3 (radio); RTE (television and radio); BBC Radio 4 ("Woman's Hour").

I wish to thank the Irish Arts Council and The Ingram Merrill Foundation for grants which assisted me in the completion of this work.

FOR KEVIN CASEY

CONTENTS

PART ONE

I
Object Lessons

II
Outside History

III
Distances

PART TWO

I
The Journey

I I
D o m e s t i c   I n t e r i o r

PART
ONE

I

Object
Lessons

THE BLACK LACE FAN
MY MOTHER GAVE ME

It was the first gift he ever gave her,
buying it for five francs in the Galeries
in prewar Paris. It was stifling.
A starless drought made the nights stormy.

They stayed in the city for the summer.
They met in cafés. She was always early.
He was late. That evening he was later.
They wrapped the fan. He looked at his watch.

She looked down the Boulevard des Capucines.
She ordered more coffee. She stood up.
The streets were emptying. The heat was killing.
She thought the distance smelled of rain and lightning.

These are wild roses, appliqued on silk by hand,
darkly picked, stitched boldly, quickly.
The rest is tortoiseshell and has the reticent,
clear patience of its element. It is

a worn-out underwater bullion and it keeps,
even now, an inference of its violation.
The lace is overcast as if the weather
it opened for and offset had entered it.

The past is an empty café terrace.
An airless dusk before thunder. A man running.
And no way now to know what happened then—
none at all—unless, of course, you improvise:

the blackbird on this first sultry morning,
in summer, finding buds, worms, fruit,
feels the heat. Suddenly she puts out her wing—
the whole, full, flirtatious span of it.

THE ROOMS OF OTHER WOMEN POETS

I wonder about you: whether the blue abrasions
of daylight, falling as dusk across your page,

make you reach for the lamp. I sometimes think
I see that gesture in the way you use language.

And whether you think, as I do, that wild flowers
dried and fired on the ironstone rim of

the saucer underneath your cup are a sign of
a savage, old calligraphy: you will not have it.

The chair you use, for instance, may be cane
soaked and curled in spirals, painted white

and eloquent, or iron mesh and the table
a horizon of its own on plain, deal trestles,

bearing up unmarked, steel-cut foolscap,
a whole quire of it; when you leave I know

you look at them and you love their air of
unaggressive silence as you close the door.

The early summer, its covenant, its grace,
is everywhere: even shadows have leaves.

Somewhere you are writing or have written in
a room you came to as I come to this

room with honeyed corners, the interior sunless,
the windows shut but clear so I can see

the bay windbreak, the laburnum hang fire, feel
the ache of things ending in the jasmine darkening early.

It was yours.
Your coffee mug. Black,
with a hunting scene on the side
(cruel theater as the kettle poured).
Together, we unpacked it
in the new house.

A hunting scene:
Dogs. Hawking. Silk.
Linen spread out in a meadow.
Pitchers of wine clouding in the shadow
of beech trees. Buttermilk.
A huntsman.

A wild rabbit.
A thrush ready to sing.
A lady smiling as the huntsman kissed her:
the way land looks before disaster
strikes or suffering
becomes a habit

was not a feature
of the history we knew. Now
it opened out before us, bright
as our curtainless October nights
whose street-lit glow
was second nature. Or

those mornings
we drank white coffee
and shared cake in a kitchen full of

chaos, before we knew the details of
this pastoral were merely
veiled warnings

of the shiver
of presentiment with which
we found the broken pieces of
the sparrow hawk and the kisses of
the huntsman, the pitcher
and the thrush's never

to-be-finished
aria, an untouched meal,
and the lady and the hunting horn
on the floorboards you and I had sworn
to sand down and seal
with varnish.

ON THE GIFT OF *THE BIRDS OF AMERICA*
BY JOHN JAMES AUDUBON

What you have given me is, of course, elegy: the red-shouldered
hawk in among these scattering partridges,
flustered at

such a descent, and the broad-winged one poised on the branch
of a pignut, and the pine siskin and the wren are
an inference

we follow in the plummet of the tern which appears to be,
from this angle anyway, impossibly fragile and
if we imagine

the franchise of light these camphor-colored wings opened out
once with and are at such a loss for now,
then surely this

is the nature and effect of elegy: the celebration of an element
which absence has revealed. It is
our earthliness

we love as we look at them, which we fear to lose, which we need
this rephrasing of the air,
of the ocean

to remind us of: that evening, late in May, the Clare hills were
ghostly with hawthorn. Two swans flew over us.
I can still hear

the musical insistence of their wings as they came in past
the treetops, near the lake; and we looked up,
rooted to the spot.

THE GAME

Outside my window an English spring was
summoning home its birds and a week-long fog
was tattering into wisps and rags and at last
I could see the railings when I looked out.

I was a child in a north-facing bedroom in
a strange country. I lay awake listening to
quarreling and taffeta creaking and the clattering
of queens and aces on the inlaid card table.

I played a game: I hid my face in the pillow
and put my arms around it until they thickened.
Then I was following the thaw northward and the air
was blond with frost and sunshine and below me

was only water and the shadow of flight in it
and the shape of wings under it, and in the hours
before morning I would be drawn down and drawn
down and there would be no ground under me

and no safe landing in the dawn breaking on
a room with sharp corners and surfaces on which
the red-jacketed and cruel-eyed fractions of chance
lay scattered where the players had abandoned them.

Later on I would get up and go to school in
the scalded light which fog leaves behind it;
and pray for the King in chapel and feel dumbly for
the archangels trapped in their granite hosannas.

THE SHADOW DOLL

(This was sent to the bride-to-be in Victorian times, by her dressmaker. It consisted of a procelain doll, under a dome of glass, modeling the proposed wedding dress.)

They stitched blooms from ivory tulle
to hem the oyster gleam of the veil.
They made hoops for the crinoline.

Now, in summary and neatly sewn—
a porcelain bride in an airless glamour—
the shadow doll survives its occasion.

Under glass, under wraps, it stays
even now, after all, discreet about
visits, fevers, quickenings and lusts

and just how, when she looked at
the shell-tone spray of seed pearls,
the bisque features, she could see herself

inside it all, holding less than real
stephanotis, rose petals, never feeling
satin rise and fall with the vows

I kept repeating on the night before—
astray among the cards and wedding gifts—
the coffee pots and the clocks and

the battered tan case full of cotton
lace and tissue paper, pressing down, then
pressing down again. And then, locks.

THE RIVER

You brought me
    to the mouth of a river
in mid-October
    when the swamp maples
were saw-toothed and blemished.
    I remember

how strange it felt—
    not having any
names for the red oak
    and the rail
and the slantways plunge
    of the osprey.

What we said was less
    than what we saw.
What we saw was
    a duck boat, slowly
passing us, a hunter and
    his spaniel and

his gun poised,
    and, in the distance,
the tips of the wild
    rice drowning in
that blue which raids and
    excludes light.

MOUNTAIN TIME

Time is shadowless there: mornings reoccur
only as enchantments, only as time for her

to watch berries ripen by on the mountain ash;
for him, at a short distance from her, to catch fish.

Afterwards, darkness will be only what is left of
a mouth after kissing or a hand laced in a hand;

a branch; a river; will be what is lost of words
as they turn to silences and then to sleep. Yet

when they leave the mountain what he will remember is
the rowan tree: that blemish, that scarlet. She will think of

the arc of the salmon after sudden capture—
its glitter a larceny of daylight on slate.

BRIGHT-CUT IRISH SILVER

I take it down
from time to time, to feel
the smooth path of silver meet the cicatrix of skill.

These scars, I tell myself, are learned.

This gift for wounding an artery of rock
was passed on from father to son, to the father
of the next son.

Is an aptitude for injuring
earth while inferring it in curves and surfaces.

Is this cold potency which has come—
by time and chance—

into my hands.

This warm, late summer there is so much
to get in. The ladder waits by the crab apple tree.
The greenhouse is rank with the best
Irish tomatoes. Pears are ripening.

Your husband frowns at dinner, has no time
for the baby who has learned to crease three
fingers and wave "day-day." This is serious,
he says. This could be what we all feared.

You pierce a sequin with a needle.
You slide it down single-knotted thread
until it lies with all the others in
a puzzle of brightness. Then another and another one.

Let the green and amber marrows rise up
and beat against it and the crab apples and
the damson-colored pram by the back
wall: you will not sew them into it.

The wooden ledge of the conservatory
faces south. Row on row,
the pears are laid out there, are hard
and then yellow and then yellow with

a rosiness. You leave them out of it.
They will grow soft and bruised at the top
and rot, all in one afternoon. The light,
which made them startling, you will use.

On the breakfast table the headlines are
telling of a city under threat where

you mixed cheese with bitter fennel and
fell in love over demitasse. Afterwards,

you walked by the moonlit river and stopped
and looked down. A glamorous circumference is
spinning on your needle, is
that moon in satin water making

the same preemptory demands on
the waves of the Irish sea and as each
salt-window opens to reveal
a weather of agates, you will stitch that in

with the orchard colors of the first preserves
you make from the garden. You move the jars from
the pantry to the windowsill where
you can see them; winter jewels.

The night he comes to tell you this is war
you wait for him to put on his dinner jacket.
The party is tonight.
The streets are quiet. Dublin is at peace.

The talk is of death but you take
the hand of the first man who asks you.
You dance the fox-trot, the two-step,
the quickstep,

in time to the music. Exclusions
glitter at your hips and past and future are
the fended-off and farfetched
in waltz time below your waist.

II

Outside History
A sequence

1
THE ACHILL WOMAN

She came up the hill carrying water.
She wore a half-buttoned, wool cardigan,
a tea-towel round her waist.

She pushed the hair out of her eyes with
her free hand and put the bucket down.

The zinc-music of the handle on the rim
tuned the evening. An Easter moon rose.
In the next-door field a stream was
a fluid sunset; and then, stars.

I remember the cold rosiness of her hands.
She bent down and blew on them like broth.
And round her waist, on a white background,
in coarse, woven letters, the words "glass cloth."

And she was nearly finished for the day.
And I was all talk, raw from college—
weekending at a friend's cottage
with one suitcase and the set text
of the Court poets of the Silver Age.

We stayed putting down time until
the evening turned cold without warning.
She said goodnight and started down the hill.

The grass changed from lavender to black.
The trees turned back to cold outlines.
You could taste frost

but nothing now can change the way I went
indoors, chilled by the wind

and made a fire
and took down my book
and opened it and failed to comprehend

the harmonies of servitude,
the grace music gives to flattery
and language borrows from ambition—

and how I fell asleep
oblivious to

the planets clouding over in the skies,
the slow decline of the spring moon,
the songs crying out their ironies.

2
A FALSE SPRING

Alders are tasseled.
Flag-iris is already out on the canal.

From my window I can see
the College gardens, crocuses stammering
in pools of rain, plum blossom on
the branches.

I want to find her,
the woman I once was, who came out of that reading room
in a hard January, after studying
Aeneas in the underworld,
how his old battle-foes spotted him there—

how they called and called and called
only to have it be
a yell of shadows, an O vanishing in
the polished waters
and the topsy-turvy seasons of hell;

her mind so frail her body was its ghost.

I want to tell her she can rest,
she is embodied now.

But narcissi,
opening too early,
are all I find. I hear the bad sound of these south winds,
the rain coming from some region which has lost sight of
our futures, leaving us
nothing to look forward to except
what one serious frost can accomplish.

3

THE MAKING OF AN
IRISH GODDESS

Ceres went to hell
with no sense of time.

When she looked back
all that she could see was

the arteries of silver in the rock,
the diligence of rivers always at one level,
wheat at one height,
leaves of a single color,
the same distance in the usual light;

a seasonless, unscarred earth.

But I need time—
my flesh and that history—
to make the same descent.

In my body,
neither young now nor fertile,
and with the marks of childbirth
still on it,

in my gestures—
the way I pin my hair to hide
the stitched, healed blemish of a scar—
must be

an accurate inscription
of that agony:

the failed harvests,
the fields rotting to the horizon,

the children devoured by their mothers
whose souls, they would have said,
went straight to hell,
followed by their own.

There is no other way:

Myth is the wound we leave
in the time we have—

which in my case is this
March evening
at the foothills of the Dublin mountains,
across which the lights have changed all day,

holding up my hand
sickle-shaped, to my eyes
to pick out
my own daughter from
all the other children in the distance;

her back turned to me.

4

WHITE HAWTHORN IN THE WEST OF IRELAND

I drove west
in the season between seasons.
I left behind suburban gardens.
Lawnmowers. Small talk.

Under low skies, past splashes of coltsfoot
I assumed
the hard shyness of Atlantic light
and the superstitious aura of hawthorn.

All I wanted then was to fill my arms with
sharp flowers,
to seem, from a distance, to be part of
that ivory, downhill rush. But I knew,

I had always known
the custom was
not to touch hawthorn.
Not to bring it indoors for the sake of

the luck
such constraint would forfeit—
a child might die, perhaps, or an unexplained
fever speckle heifers. So I left it

stirring on those hills
with a fluency
only water has. And, like water, able
to redefine land. And free to seem to be—

for anglers,
and for travelers astray in
the unmarked lights of a May dusk—
the only language spoken in those parts.

DAPHNE HEARD WITH HORROR THE ADDRESSES OF THE GOD

It was early summer. Already
the conservatory was all steam and greenness.
I would have known the stephanotis by
its cutthroat sweetness anywhere.
We drank tea. You were telling me
a story you had heard as a child,
about the wedding of a local girl,
long ago, and a merchant from Argyll.

I thought the garden looked so at ease.
The roses were beginning on one side.
The laurel hedge was nothing but itself,
and all of it so free of any need
for nymphs, goddesses, wounded presences—
the fleet river-daughters who took root
and can be seen in the woods in
unmistakable shapes of weeping.

You were still speaking. By the time
I paid attention they were well married:
The bridegroom had his bride on the ship.
The sails were ready to be set. You said
small craft went with her to the ship, and
as it sailed out, well-wishers
took in armfuls, handfuls, from the boats
white roses and threw them on the water.

We cleared up then, saying how
the greenfly needed spraying, the azaleas
were over; and you went inside. I
stayed in the heat looking out at

the garden in its last definition,
freshening and stirring. A suggestion,
behind it all, of darkness: in the shadow,
beside the laurel hedge, its gesture.

6

THE PHOTOGRAPH ON MY
FATHER'S DESK

It could be
any summer afternoon.

The sun is warm on
the fruitwood garden seat.
Fuchsia droops.
Thrushes move to get
windfalls underneath the crab apple tree.

The woman
holds her throat like a wound.

She wears
mutton-colored gaberdine with
a scum of lace
just above her boot

which is pointed at
this man coming down the path with
his arms wide open. Laughing.

The garden fills up
with a burned silence.

The talk has stopped.
The spoon which just now
jingled at the rim of the lemonade jug
is still.

And the shrubbed lavender
will find
neither fragrance nor muslin.

7

WE ARE HUMAN HISTORY.
WE ARE NOT NATURAL HISTORY.

At twilight in
the shadow of the poplars
the children found a swarm of wild bees.

It was late summer and I knew as
they came shouting in that, yes,
this evening had been singled out by

a finger pointing at trees,
the inland feel of that greenness,
the sugar-barley iron of a garden chair

and children still bramble-height
and fretful from the heat and a final
brightness stickle-backing that particular

patch of grass across which light
was short-lived and elegiac as
the view from a train window of

a station parting, all tears. And this—
this I thought, is how it will have been
chosen from those summer evenings

which under the leaves of the poplars—
striped dun and ochre, simmering over
the stashed-up debris of old seasons—

a swarm of wild bees is making use of.

AN OLD STEEL ENGRAVING

Look.
The figure in the foreground breaks his fall with
one hand. He cannot die.
The river cannot wander
into the shadows to be dragged by willows.
The passerby is scared witless. He cannot escape.
He cannot stop staring at
this hand which can barely raise
the patriot
above the ground, which is
the origin and reason for it all.

patriot - to love of defend one's country

malediction - a curse that invokes evil

More closely now:
at the stillness of unfinished action in
afternoon heat, at the spaces on the page. They widen
to include us:
we have found
the country of our malediction where
nothing can move until we find the word,
nothing can stir until we say this is
what happened and is happening and history
is one of us who turns away,
while the other is
turning the page.

Morse - words/ telegraph code represented by dots and dashes

| = no pause

Is this river which
moments ago must have flashed the morse
of a bayonet thrust. And is moving on.

IN EXILE

The German girls who came to us that winter and
the winter after and who helped my mother fuel
the iron stove and arranged our clothes in wet
thicknesses on the wooden rail after tea was over,

spoke no English, understood no French. They were
sisters from a ruined city and they spoke rapidly
in their own tongue: syllables in which pain was
radical, integral; and with what sense of injury

the language angled for an unhurt kingdom—for
the rise, curve, kill and swift return to the wrist,
to the hood—I never knew. To me they were the sounds
of evening only, of the cold, of the Irish dark and

continuous with all such recurrences: the drizzle in
the lilac, the dusk always at the back door, like
the tinkers I was threatened with, the cat inching
closer to the fire with its screen of clothes, where

I am standing in the stone-flagged kitchen; there are
bleached rags, perhaps, and a pot of tea on the stove.
And I see myself, four years of age and looking up,
storing such music—guttural, hurt to the quick—

as I hear now, forty years on and far from where
I heard it first. Among these saltboxes, marshes and
the glove-tanned colors of the sugar maples, in
this New England town at the start of winter, I am

so much south of it: the soft wet, the light and
those early darks which strengthen the assassin's
hand; and hide the wound. Here, in this scalding air,
my speech will not heal. I do not want it to heal.

WE ARE ALWAYS TOO LATE

Memory
is in two parts.

First, the revisiting:

the way even now I can see
those lovers at the café table. She is weeping.

It is New England, breakfast time, winter. Behind her,
outside the picture window, is
a stand of white pines.

New snow falls and the old,
losing its balance in the branches,
showers down,
adding fractions to it. Then

the reenactment. Always that.
I am getting up, pushing away
coffee. Always, I am going towards her.

The flush and scald is
to her forehead now, and back down to her neck.

I raise one hand. I am pointing to
those trees, I am showing her our need for these
beautiful upstagings of
what we suffer by
what survives. And she never even sees me.

WHAT WE LOST

It is a winter afternoon.
The hills are frozen. Light is failing.
The distance is a crystal earshot.
A woman is mending linen in her kitchen.

She is a countrywoman.
Behind her cupboard doors she hangs sprigged,
stove-dried lavender in muslin.
Her letters and mementos and memories

are packeted in satin at the back with
gaberdine and worsted and
the cambric she has made into bodices;
the good tobacco silk for Sunday Mass.

She is sewing in the kitchen.
The sugar-feel of flax is in her hands.
Dusk. And the candles brought in then.
One by one. And the quiet sweat of wax.

There is a child at her side.
The tea is poured, the stitching put down.
The child grows still, sensing something of importance.
The woman settles and begins her story.

Believe it, what we lost is here in this room
on this veiled evening.
The woman finishes. The story ends.
The child, who is my mother, gets up, moves away.

In the winter air, unheard, unshared,
the moment happens, hangs fire, leads nowhere.
The light will fail and the room darken,
the child fall asleep and the story be forgotten.

The fields are dark already.
The frail connections have been made and are broken.
The dumb-show of legend has become language,
is becoming silence and who will know that once

words were possibilities and disappointments,
were scented closets filled with love letters
and memories and lavender hemmed into muslin,
stored in sachets, aired in bed linen;

and traveled silks and the tones of cotton
tautened into bodices, subtly shaped by breathing;
were the rooms of childhood with their griefless peace,
their hands and whispers, their candles weeping brightly?

OUTSIDE HISTORY

There are outsiders, always. These stars—
these iron inklings of an Irish January,
whose light happened

thousands of years before
our pain did: they are, they have always been
outside history.

They keep their distance. Under them remains
a place where you found
you were human, and

a landscape in which you know you are mortal.
And a time to choose between them.
I have chosen:

Out of myth into history I move to be
part of that ordeal
whose darkness is

only now reaching me from those fields,
those rivers, those roads clotted as
firmaments with the dead.

How slowly they die
as we kneel beside them, whisper in their ear.
And we are too late. We are always too late.

III

Distances

THE LATIN LESSON

Easter light in the convent garden.
The eucalyptus tree glitters in it.
       A bell rings for
       the first class.

Today the Sixth Book of the *Aeneid*.
An old nun calls down the corridor.
       Manners, girls. Where
       are your manners?

Last night in his Lenten talk
the local priest asked us to remember
       everything is put here
       for a purpose:

even eucalyptus leaves are suitable
for making oil from to steep wool in,
       to sweeten our blankets
       and gaberdines.

My forefinger crawls on the lines.
A storm light comes in from the bay.
       How beautiful the words
       look, how

vagrant and strange on the page
before we crush them for their fragrance
       and crush them again
       to discover

the pathway to hell and that these
shadows in their shadow-bodies,

chittering and mobbing
on the far

shore, signaling their hunger for
the small usefulness of a life are
the dead and how
before the bell

will I hail the black keel and flatter the dark
boatman and cross the river and still
keep a civil tongue
in my head?

My mother kept a stockpot—

garlic cloves, bones,
rinds, pearl onions and the lacy spine and eyes
of a trout went into it—

When the window cleared, the garden showed
beyond the lemon balm,
through the steam,
cats:

Bucking. Rutting.
All buttocks and stripes.
Up on the wall and wild, they made the garden wild—
for all the gelded shrubs and the careful stemming
on trellises, of a bushed-out, pastel clematis.

One summer night I went out to them.
I looked up. Their eyes looked back—

not the color of fields or kale—
the available greens—
but jade-cold
and with a closed-in chill I was used to—

lucid as a nursery rhyme and as hard to fathom,
revealed by rhythm, belied by theme,
never forgotten

in those nights of childhood
in a roomful of breathing, under wartime sheeting.

Outside, the screams and stridency of mating.

THE CAROUSEL IN THE PARK

Find it.

Down the park walks, on the path leading
past the sycamores.
There through the trees—

nasturtium rumps, breasts plunging
lime and violet manes
painted on
what was once the same as now littered
russet on their petrified advance.

Find the sun
in the morning rising later,
the chilled afternoons getting shorter and—
after dusk, in the lake, in the park—
the downtown city windows scattering
a galaxy of money
in the water.

And winter coming:
The manhandled indigo necks flexing and
the flared noses
and the heads with their quiffed carving.
And the walks leafless and
the squirrels gone,
the sycamores bare and the lake frozen.

Find the child,
going high and descending there—up and down,
up, down again—

her mittens bright as finger-paints and holding fast
to a crust of weather now: twelve years of age in
a thigh-length coat,
unable to explain a sense of ease in

those safe curves, that seasonless canter.

CONTINGENCIES

Waiting in the kitchen for power cuts,
on this wet night, sorting candles,
feeling the tallow,
brings back to me
the way women spoke in my childhood—

with a sweet mildness in front of company,
or with a private hunger in whispered kisses
or with the crisis-bright words
which meant

you and you alone were their object—

"Stop that." "Wait till I get you."
"Dry those tears."

I stand the candles in jam jars
lined in a row on the table,
scalded and dried with a glass cloth;

which all last summer were crammed with
the fruits of neighborly gardens;

stoned plums and damsons, loganberries.

SPRING AT THE EDGE
OF THE SONNET

Late March and I'm still lighting fires—

last night's frost which killed the new
shoots of ivy in the terra-cotta churn,
has turned the fields of wheat and winter barley

to icy slates on the hills rising
outside the windows of our living room.

Still, there are signs of change. Soon,
the roofs of cars, which last month were
oracles of ice and unthawed dawns,

will pass by, veiled in blooms from
the wild plum they parked under overnight.

Last night, as I drove from town,
the dark was in and the lovers were
out in doorways, using them as windbreaks,
making shadows seem nothing more than

sweet exchequers for a homeless kiss.

OUR ORIGINS ARE IN THE SEA

I live near the coast. On these summer nights
Arcturus is already there, steadfast
in the southeast. I stand at the edge of our grass.

I do not connect them: once they were connected—
the fixity of stars and unruly salt water—
by sailors with an avarice for landfall.

And this is land. The way the whitebeams will
begin their fall to an alluvial earth and
a bicycle wheel is spinning on it, proves that.

From where I stand the sea is just a rumor.
The stars are put out by our street lamp. Light
and seawater are well separated. And how little

survives of the sea captain in his granddaughter
is everywhere apparent. Such things get lost:
He drowned in the Bay of Biscay. I never saw him.

I turn to go in. The hills are indistinct.
The coast is near and darkening. The stars are clearer.
The grass and the house are lapped in shadow.

And the briar rose is rigged in the twilight,
the way I imagine sails used to be—
lacy and stiff together, a frigate of ivory.

I go down step by step.
The house is quiet, full of trapped heat and sleep.
In the kitchen everything is still.
Nothing is distinct; there is no moon to speak of.

I could be undone every single day by
paradox or what they call in the countryside
blackthorn winter,
when hailstones come with the first apple blossom.

I turn a switch and the garden grows.
A whole summer's work in one instant!
I press my face to the glass. I can see
shadows of lilac, of fuchsia; a dark likeness of blackcurrant:

little clients of suddenness, how sullen they are at
the margins of the light.
They need no rain, they have no roots.
I reach out a hand; they are gone.

When I was a child a snapdragon was
held an inch from my face. Look, a voice said, this
is the color of your hair. And there it was, my head,
a pliant jewel in the hands of someone else.

DOORSTEP KISSES

The white iron of the garden chair is
the only thing dusk makes clearer.

I have stumbled on
the last days of summer in the last hour of light.

If I stay here long enough I may become—
since everything else around me is—

the sum of small gestures, choices,
losses in the air so fractional
they could be

fragrances which just fell from it—

a musk of buddleia, perhaps, or this fuchsia
with the drip,
drip of whitby jet fringing
an old rose printed shawl I saw once

which swung out and over my shoulders,
flinging out its scent
of early chills and doorstep kisses.

Talking just like this late at night
all depends on a sense of mystery;
the same things in a different light.

Your whiskey glass and the watercolor
just off-center are
part of this. The electric pallor

of that apple, also. And the slow
arc of an indoor palm, the vase beside it blooming
with shadows. Do you remember how

the power cuts caught us unawares?
No candles and no torch. It was high
summer. A soft brightness clung in the poplars,

for hours it seemed. When it went out,
everything we knew how
to look for had disappeared. And when light

came back, it came back as noise:
the radio; the deep freeze singing.
Afterwards we talked of it for days—

how it felt at the upstairs window,
to stand and watch and still miss the moment
of gable ends and rooftops beginning

to be rebuilt. And that split second when
you and I were, from a distance,
a neighborhood on the verge of definition.

HANGING CURTAINS WITH AN ABSTRACT PATTERN IN A CHILD'S ROOM

I chose these for you—
not the precinct of the unicorn, nor

the half-torn
singlet of a nursery rhyme prince, but

the signals of enigma:
Ellipse. Triangle. A music of ratio.

Draw these lines
against a winter dusk. Let them stand in for

frost on the spider's web and on
bicycle sheds.

Observe
how the season enters pure line

like a soul: all the signs we know
are only ways

of coming to our senses.
I can see

the distances off-loading color now
into angles as

I hang their weather in
your room, all the time wondering

just how I look from the road—
my blouse off-white and

my skirt the color of
all the disappointments of a day when

the curtains are pulled back on
a dull morning.

GHOST STORIES

I answer
the door. In my hands are windfalls

which have sweetened on the garage shelves all this
northerly autumn,
stealthily, beside the fretsaw and spirit level.

Our American Hallowe'en was years ago. We wore
anoraks and gloves
and stood outside to watch

the moon above Iowa. Before dark
I walked

out through the parking lot and playground
to our apartment block.

On every porch, every doorstep candles fluttered in
pumpkins in the dusk on the eve
of the holiday. We

were strangers
there. I remember how our lighted rooms
looked through curtains from the road:

with that fragility.

WHAT LOVE INTENDED

I can imagine if,
I came back again,
    looking through windows at

    broken mirrors, pictures,
and, in the cracked upstairs,
    the beds where it all began.

    The suburb in the rain
this October morning
    full of food and children

    and animals, will be—
when I come back again—
    gone to rack and ruin.

    I will be its ghost,
its revenant, discovering
    again in one place

    the history of my pain,
my ordeal, my grace,
    unable to resist

    seeing what is past,
judging what has ended
    and whether, first to last,

    from then to now and even
here, ruined, this
    is what love intended—

finding even the yellow
jasmine in the dusk,
    the smell of early dinners,

    the voices of our children,
taking turns and quarreling,
    burned on the distance,

    gone. And the small square
where under cropped lime
    and poplar, on bicycles

    and skates in the summer,
they played until dark;
    propitiating time.

    And even the two whitebeams
outside the house gone,
    with the next-door neighbor

    who used to say in April—
when one was slow to bloom—
    they were a man and woman.

DISTANCES

The radio is playing downstairs in the kitchen.
The clock says eight and the light says
winter. You are pulling up your hood against a bad morning.

Don't leave, I say. Don't go without telling me
the name of that song. You call it back to me from the stairs:
"I Wish I Was In Carrickfergus"

and the words open out with emigrant grief the way the streets
of a small town open out in
memory: salt-loving fuchsias to one side and

a market in full swing on the other with
linen for sale and tacky apples and a glass and wire hill
of spectacles on a metal tray. The front door bangs

and you're gone. I will think of it all morning while a fine
drizzle closes in, making the distances
fiction: not of that place but this and of how

restless we would be, you and I, inside the perfect
music of that basalt and sandstone
coastal town. We would walk the streets in

the scentless afternoon of a ballad measure,
longing to be able
to tell each other that the starched lace and linen of

adult handkerchiefs scraped your face and left your tears
falling; how the apples were mush inside the crisp sugar
shell and the spectacles out of focus.

PART
TWO

I

The
Journey

I was standing there
at the end of a reading
or a workshop or whatever,
watching people heading
out into the weather,

only half-wondering
what becomes of words,
the brisk herbs of language,
the fragrances we think we sing,
if anything.

We were left behind
in a firelit room
in which the color scheme
crouched well down—
golds, a sort of dun

a distressed ocher—
and the sole richness was
in the suggestion of a texture
like the low flax gleam
that comes off polished leather.

Two women
were standing in shadow,
one with her back turned.
Their talk was a gesture,
an outstretched hand.

They talked to each other,
and words like "summer,"
"birth," "great-grandmother"

kept pleading with me,
urging me to follow.

"She could feel it coming"—
one of them was saying—
"all the way there,
across the fields at evening
and no one there, God help her

"and she had on a skirt
of cross-woven linen
and the little one
kept pulling at it.
It was nearly night . . ."

(Wood hissed and split
in the open grate,
broke apart in sparks,
a windfall of light
in the room's darkness)

". . . when she lay down
and gave birth to him
in an open meadow.
What a child that was
to be born without a blemish!"

It had started raining,
the windows dripping, misted.
One moment I was standing
not seeing out,
only half-listening

staring at the night; the next
without warning
I was caught by it:
the bruised summer light,

the musical subtext

of mauve eaves on lilac
and the laburnum past
and shadows where the lime
tree dropped its bracts
in frills of contrast

where she lay down
in vetch and linen
and lifted up her son
to the archive
they would shelter in:

the oral song
avid as superstition,
layered like an amber in
the wreck of language
and the remnants of a nation.

I was getting out
my coat, buttoning it,
shrugging up the collar.
It was bitter outside,
a real winter's night

and I had distances
ahead of me: iron miles
in trains, iron rails
repeating instances
and reasons; the wheels

singing innuendos, hints,
outlines underneath
the surface, a sense
suddenly of truth,
its resonance.

MISE EIRE

I won't go back to it—

my nation displaced
into old dactyls,
oaths made
by the animal tallows
of the candle—

land of the Gulf Stream,
the small farm,
the scalded memory,
the songs
that bandage up the history,
the words
that make a rhythm of the crime

where time is time past.
A palsy of regrets.
No. I won't go back.
My roots are brutal:

I am the woman—
a sloven's mix
of silk at the wrists,
a sort of dove-strut
in the precincts of the garrison—

who practices
the quick frictions,
the rictus of delight
and gets cambric for it,
rice-colored silks.

I am the woman
in the gansy-coat
on board the *Mary Belle*,
in the huddling cold,

holding her half-dead baby to her
as the wind shifts east
and north over the dirty
water of the wharf

mingling the immigrant
guttural with the vowels
of homesickness who neither
knows nor cares that

a new language
is a kind of scar
and heals after a while
into a passable imitation
of what went before.

SELF-POTRAIT ON
A SUMMER EVENING

Jean-Baptiste Chardin
is painting a woman
in the last summer light.

All summer long
he has been slighting her
in botched blues, tints,
half-tones, rinsed neutrals.

What you are watching
is light unlearning itself,
an infinite unfrocking of the prism.

Before your eyes
the ordinary life
is being glazed over:
pigments of the bibelot,
the cabochon, the water-opal
pearl to the intimate
simple colors of
her ankle-length summer skirt.

Truth makes shift:
the triptych shrinks
to the cabinet picture.

Can't you feel it?
Aren't you chilled by it?
The way the late afternoon
is reduced to detail—

the sky that odd shade of apron—
opaque, scumbled—

the lazulis of the horizon becoming
optical grays
before your eyes
before your eyes
in my ankle-length
summer skirt

crossing between
the garden and the house,
under the whitebeam trees,
keeping an eye on
the length of the grass,
the height of the hedge,
the distance of the children

I am Chardin's woman

edged in reflected light,
hardened by
the need to be ordinary.

THE GLASS KING

Isabella of Bavaria married Charles VI of France in 1385. In
later years his madness took the form of believing he was
made from glass.

When he is ready he is raised and carried
among his vaporish plants; the palms and ferns flex;
they almost bend; you'd almost think they were going to kiss him,
and so they might; but she will not, his wife,

no she can't kiss his lips in case he splinters
into a million Bourbons, mad pieces.
What can she do with him—her daft prince?
His nightmares are the Regency of France.

Yes, she's been through it all, his Bavaroise,
blub-hipped and docile, urgent to be needed—
from churching to milk fever, from tongue-tied princess
to the queen of a mulish king—and now this.

They were each other's fantasy in youth.
No splintering at all about that mouth
when they were flesh and muscle, woman and man,
fire and kindling? See that silk divan?

Enough said. Now the times themselves
are his asylum: these are the Middle Ages, sweet
and savage era of the saving grace; indulgences
are two a penny; under the stonesmith's hand

stone turns into lace. I need his hand now.
Outside my window October soaks the stone;
you can hear it; you'd almost think
the brick was drinking it; the rowan drips

and history waits. Let it wait. I want
no elsewheres: the clover-smelling, stove-warm
air of Autumn catches cold; the year turns;
the leaves fall; the poem hesitates:

If we could see ourselves, not as we do—
in mirrors, self-deceptions, self-regardings—
but as we ought to be and as we have been:
poets, lute-stringers, makyres and abettors

of our necessary art, soothsayers of the ailment
and disease of our times, sweet singers,
truth tellers, intercessors for self-knowledge—
what would we think of these fin-de-siècle

half-hearted penitents we have become
at the sick bed of the century: hand-wringing
elegists with an ill-concealed greed
for the inheritance?
                              My prince, demented

in a crystal past, a lost France, I elect you emblem
and ancestor of our lyric: it fits you like a glove—
doesn't it?—the part; untouchable, outlandish,
esoteric, inarticulate and out of reach

of human love: studied every day by your wife,
an ordinary, honest woman out of place
in all this, wanting nothing more than the man
she married, all her sorrows in her stolid face.

THE WOMEN

This is the hour I love: the in-between
neither here-nor-there hour of evening.
The air is tea-colored in the garden.
The briar rose is spilled crepe de Chine.

This is the time I do my work best,
going up the stairs in two minds,
in two worlds, carrying cloth or glass,
leaving something behind, bringing
something with me I should have left behind.

The hour of change, of metamorphosis,
of shape-shifting instabilities.
My time of sixth sense and second sight
when in the words I choose, the lines I write,
they rise like visions and appear to me:

women of work, of leisure, of the night,
in stove-colored silks, in lace, in nothing,
with crewel needles, with books, with wide-open legs,

who fled the hot breath of the god pursuing,
who ran from the split hoof and the thick lips
and fell and grieved and healed into myth,

into me in the evening at my desk
testing the water with a sweet quartet,
the physical force of a dissonance—

the fission of music into syllabic heat—
and getting sick of it and standing up
and going downstairs in the last brightness

into a landscape without emphasis,
light, linear, precisely planned,
a hemisphere of tiered, aired cotton,

a hot terrain of linen from the iron,
folded in and over, stacked high,
neatened flat, stoving heat and white.

THE BRIAR ROSE

Intimate as underthings
beside the matronly damasks—

the last thing
to go out at night
is the lanternlike, white insistence
of these small flowers;

their camisole glow.

Standing here on the front step
watching wildness break out again

it could be
the unlighted stairway,
I could be
the child I was, opening

a bedroom door
on Irish whiskey, lipstick,
an empty glass,
oyster crepe de Chine

and closing it without knowing why.

FEVER

is what remained or what they thought
remained after the ague and the sweats
were over and the shock of wild flowers
at the bedside had been taken away;

is what they tried to shake out of
the crush and dimple of cotton,
the shy dust of a bridal skirt;
is what they beat, hurt, lashed like

flesh as if it were a lack of virtue
in a young girl sobbing her heart out
in a small town for having been seen
kissing by the river; is what they burned

alive in their own back gardens
as if it were a witch and not the full-
length winter gaberdine and breathed again
when the fires went out in charred dew.

My grandmother died in a fever ward,
younger than I am and far from
the sweet chills of a Louth spring—
its sprigged light and its wild flowers—

with five orphan daughters to her name.
Names and shadows, visitations, hints
and a half-sense of half-lives remain;
and nothing else, nothing more unless

I reconstruct the soaked-through midnights;
brokenhearted vigils; the histories I never learned

to predict the lyric of; and reconstruct
risk: as if silence could become rage,

as if what we lost is a contagion
that breaks out in what cannot be
shaken out from words or beaten out
from meaning and survives to weaken

what is given, what is certain
and burns away everything but this
exact moment of delirium when
someone cries out someone's name.

LACE

Bent over
the open notebook—

light fades out
making the trees stand out
and my room
at the back
of the house, dark.

In the dusk
I am still
looking for it—
the language that is

lace:

a baroque obligation
at the wrist
of a prince
in a petty court.
Look, just look
at the way he shakes out

the thriftless phrases
the crystal rhetoric
of bobbined knots
and bosses:
a vagrant drift
of emphasis
to wave away an argument
or frame the hand
he kisses;
which, for all that, is still

what someone
in the corner
of a room,
in the dusk,
bent over
as the light was fading

lost their sight for.

THE UNLIVED LIFE

"Listen to me," I said to my neighbor,
"how do you make a hexagon-shape template?"

So we talked about end papers,
cropped circles, block piecework
while the children shouted and
the texture of synthetics as compared
with the touch of strong cloth;
and how they both washed.

"You start out with jest so much caliker,"
Eliza Calvert Hall of Kentucky said—
"that's the predestination
but when it comes to cuttin' out
the quilt, why you're free to choose."

Suddenly I could see us
calicoed, overawed, dressed in cotton
at the railroad crossing, watching
the flange-wheeled, steam-driven, iron omen
of another life passing, passing,
wondering for a moment what it was
we were missing as we turned for home—

to choose
in the shiver of silk and dimity
the unlived life, its symmetry
explored on a hoop with a crewel needle
under the silence of the oil light;

to formalize the terrors of routine
in the algebras of a marriage quilt
on alternate mornings when you knew

that all you owned was what you shared.

It was bedtime for the big children
and long past it for the little ones
as we turned to go
and the height of the season went by us;

tendrils, leaps, gnarls of blossom,
asteroids and day stars of our small world,
the sweet pea ascending the trellis
the clematis descended
as day backed into night
and separate darks blended the shadows,
singling a star out of thin air

as we went in.

THE JOURNEY
FOR ELIZABETH RYLE

Immediately cries were heard. These were the loud wailing of infant souls at the very entranceway; never had they had their share of life's sweetness for the dark day had stolen them from their mothers' breasts and plunged them to a death before their time.

Vergil, The Aeneid, Book VI

And then the dark fell and "there has never"
I said "been a poem to an antibiotic:
never a word to compare with the odes on
the flower of the raw sloe for fever

"or the devious Africa-seeking tern
or the protein treasures of the sea bed.
Depend on it, somewhere a poet is wasting
his sweet uncluttered meters on the obvious

"emblem instead of the real thing.
Instead of sulpha we shall have hyssop dipped
in the wild blood of the unblemished lamb,
so every day the language gets less

"for the task and we are less with the language."
I finished speaking and the anger faded
and dark fell and the book beside me
lay open at the page Aphrodite

comforts Sappho in her love's duress.
The poplars shifted their music in the garden,
a child startled in a dream,
my room was a mess—

the usual hardcovers, half-finished cups,
clothes piled up on an old chair—
and I was listening out but in my head was
a loosening and sweetening heaviness,

not sleep, but nearly sleep, not dreaming really
but as ready to believe and still
unfevered, calm and unsurprised
when she came and stood beside me

and I would have known her anywhere
and I would have gone with her anywhere
and she came wordlessly
and without a word I went with her

down down down without so much as
ever touching down but always, always
with a sense of mulch beneath us,
the way of stairs winding down to a river

and as we went on the light went on
failing and I looked sideways to be certain
it was she, misshapen, musical—
Sappho—the scholiast's nightingale

and down we went, again down
until we came to a sudden rest
beside a river in what seemed to be
an oppressive suburb of the dawn.

My eyes got slowly used to the bad light.
At first I saw shadows, only shadows.
Then I could make out women and children
and, in the way they were, the grace of love.

"Cholera, typhus, croup, diptheria,"
she said, "in those days they racketed
in every backstreet and alley of old Europe.
Behold the children of the plague."

Then to my horror I could see to each
nipple some had clipped a limpet shape—

suckling darknesses—while others had their arms
weighed down, making terrible pietas.

She took my sleeve and said to me "be careful.
Do not define these women by their work:
not as washerwomen trussed in dust and sweating,
muscling water into linen by the river's edge

"nor as court ladies brailled in silk
on wool, and woven with an ivory unicorn
and hung, nor as laundresses tossing cotton,
brisking daylight with lavender and gossip.

"But these are women who went out like you
when dusk became a dark sweet with leaves,
recovering the day, stooping, picking up
teddy bears and rag dolls and tricycles and buckets—

"love's archaeology—and they too like you
stood boot deep in flowers once in summer
or saw winter come in with a single magpie
in a caul of haws, a solo harlequin."

I stood fixed. I could not reach or speak to them.
Between us was the melancholy river,
the dream water, the narcotic crossing.
They had passed over it, its cold persuasions.

I whispered, "let me be
let me at least be their witness," but she said
"what you have seen is beyond speech,
beyond song, only not beyond love;

"remember it, you will remember it"
and I heard her say but she was fading fast
as we emerged under the stars of heaven,
"there are not many of us; you are dear

"and stand beside me as my own daughter.
I have brought you here so you will know forever
the silences in which are our beginnings,
in which we have an origin like water,"

and the wind shifted and the window clasp
opened, banged and I woke up to find
my poetry books spread higgledy-piggledy,
my skirt spread out where I had laid it—

nothing was changed; nothing was more clear
but it was wet and the year was late.
The rain was grief in arrears; my children
slept the last dark out safely and I wept.

ENVOI

It is Easter in the suburb. Clematis
shrubs the eaves and trellises with pastel.
The evenings lengthen and before the rain
the Dublin mountains become visible.

My muse must be better than those of men
who made theirs in the image of their myth.
The work is half-finished and I have nothing
but the crudest measures to complete it with.

Under the street lamps the dustbins brighten.
The winter-flowering jasmine casts a shadow
outside my window in my neighbor's garden.
These are the things that my muse must know.

She must come to me. Let her come
to be among the donnée, the given.
I need her to remain with me until
the day is over and the song is proven.

Surely she comes, surely she comes to me—
no lizard skin, no paps, no podded womb
about her but a brightening and
the consequences of an April tomb.

What I have done I have done alone.
What I have seen is unverified.
I have the truth and I need the faith.
It is time I put my hand in her side.

If she will not bless the ordinary,
if she will not sanctify the common,
then here I am and here I stay and then am I
the most miserable of women.

SUBURBAN WOMAN: A DETAIL

I

The chimneys have been swept.
The gardens have their winter cut.
The shrubs are prinked, the hedges gelded.

The last dark shows up the headlights
of the cars coming down the Dublin mountains.

Our children used to think they were stars.

II

This is not the season
when the goddess rose
out of seed, out of wheat,
out of thawed water
and went, distracted and astray,
to find her daughter.

Winter will be soon:
dun pools of rain;
ruddy, addled distances;
winter pinks, tinges and
a first-thing smell of turf
when I take the milk in.

III

Setting out for a neighbor's house
in a denim skirt,

a blouse blended in
by the last light,

I am definite
to start with
but the light is lessening,
the hedge losing its detail,
the path its edge.

Look at me, says the tree.
I was a woman once like you,
full-skirted, human.

Suddenly I am not certain
of the way I came
or the way I will return,
only that something
which may be nothing
more than darkness has begun
softening the definitions of my body, leaving

the fears
and all the terrors of the flesh,
shifting the airs and forms
of the autumn quiet,

crying "remember us."

I REMEMBER

I remember the way the big windows washed
out the room and the winter darks tinted
it and how, in the brute quiet and aftermath,
an eyebrow waited helplessly to be composed

from the palette with its scarabs of oil
colors gleaming through a dusk leaking from
the iron railings and the ruined evenings of
bombed-out, postwar London; how the easel was

mulberry wood and, porcupining in a jar,
the spines of my mother's portrait brushes
spiked from the dirty turpentine and the face
on the canvas was the scattered fractions

of the face which had come up the stairs
that morning and had taken up position in
the big drawing room and had been still
and was now gone; and I remember, I remember

I was the interloper who knows both love and fear,
who comes near and draws back, who feels nothing
beyond the need to touch, to handle, to dismantle it
the mystery; and how in the morning when I came down—

a nine-year-old in high fawn socks—
the room had been shocked into a glacier
of cotton sheets thrown over the almond
and vanilla silk of the French Empire chairs.

THE BOTTLE GARDEN

I decanted them—feather mosses, fan-shaped plants,
asymmetric grays in the begonia—
into this globe which shows up how the fern shares
the invertebrate lace of the seahorse.

The sun is in the bottle garden,
submarine, out of its element,
when I come down on a spring morning;
my sweet, greenish, inland underwater.

And in my late thirties, past the middle way,
I can say how did I get here?
I hardly know the way back, still less forward.
Still, if you look for them there are signs:

earth stars, rock spleenwort, creeping fig
and English ivy all furled and herded
into the green and cellar wet
of the bottle; well, here they are

here I am a gangling schoolgirl
in the convent library, the April evening outside,
reading *The Aeneid* as the room darkens
to the underworld of the sixth book—

the Styx, the damned, the pity and
the improvised poetic of imprisoned meanings;
only half aware of the open weave of harbor lights
and my school blouse riding up at the sleeves.

GROWING-UP

from Renoir's drawing *Girlhood*

Their two heads, hatted, bowed,
mooning above their waist-high
tides of hair, pair hopes.

This is the haul and full of fantasy:
full-skirted girls,
a canvas blued with a view of
unschemed space and the anemic quick
of a pencil picking out
dreams blooding them with womanhood.

They face the future. If they only knew!

There in the distance, bonneted,
round as the hairline of a child—
indefinite and infinite with hope—
is the horizon, is the past and all
they look forward to is memory.

SARAH ON HOLIDAY

Ballyvaughan; peat and salt.
The wind bawls across these mountains,
scalds the orchids
of the Burren.

They used to leave milk out once
on these windowsills,
to ward away
child-stealing spirits.

The sheets are damp.
We sleep between the blankets.
The light cotton of the curtains
lets the light in.

You wake first thing
and in your five-year-size
striped nightie you are
everywhere, trying everything:
the springs on the bed,
the hinges on the windows.

You know your a's and b's;
but there's a limit now
to what you'll believe.

When dark comes I leave
a superstitious feast of
wheat biscuits, apples,
orange juice out for you;

and wake to find it eaten.

CANALETTO IN THE NATIONAL GALLERY OF IRELAND

Something beating in
making pain and attention—
a heat still
livid on the skin
is the might-have-been:

the nation, the city
which fell
for want of
the elevation in
this view of the Piazza,

its everyday light
making it everyone's
remembered city:
airs and shadows,
cambered distances.

I remember a city
like this—
the static coral
of reflected brick
in its river.

I envy these
pinpointed citizens
their complacency,
their lack of any need
to come and see

Citizens come and see?

a beloved republic
raised and
saved and
scalded into
something measurable.

AN IRISH CHILDHOOD
IN ENGLAND : 1951

The bickering of vowels on the buses,
the clicking thumbs and the big hips of
the navy-skirted ticket collectors with
their crooked seams brought it home to me:

Exile. Ration-book pudding.
Bowls of dripping and the fixed smile
of the school pianist playing "Iolanthe,"
"Land of Hope and Glory" and "John Peel."

I didn't know what to hold, to keep.
At night, filled with some malaise
of love for what I'd never known I had,
I fell asleep and let the moment pass.

The passing moment has become a night
of clipped shadows, freshly painted houses,
the garden eddying in dark and heat,
my children half-awake, half-asleep.

Airless, humid dark. Leaf-noise.
The stirrings of a garden before rain.
A hint of storm behind the risen moon.
We are what we have chosen. Did I choose to?—

in a strange city, in another country,
on nights in a north-facing bedroom,
waiting for the sleep that never did
restore me as I'd hoped to what I'd lost—

let the world I knew become the space
between the words that I had by heart

and all the other speech that always was
becoming the language of the country that

I came to in nineteen fifty-one:
barely-gelled, a freckled six-year-old,
overdressed and sick on the plane,
when all of England to an Irish child

was nothing more than what you'd lost and how:
was the teacher in the London convent who,
when I produced "I amn't" in the classroom
turned and said—"you're not in Ireland now."

THE EMIGRANT IRISH

Like oil lamps, we put them out the back—

of our houses, of our minds. We had lights
better than, newer than and then

a time came, this time and now
we need them. Their dread, makeshift example:

they would have thrived on our necessities.
What they survived we could not even live.
By their lights now it is time to
imagine how they stood there, what they stood with,
that their possessions may become our power:

Cardboard. Iron. Their hardships parceled in them.
Patience. Fortitude. Long-suffering
in the bruise-colored dusk of the New World.

And all the old songs. And nothing to lose.

FOND MEMORY

It was a school where all the children wore darned worsted,
where they cried—or almost all—when the Reverend Mother
announced at lunchtime that the King had died

peacefully in his sleep. I dressed in wool as well,
ate rationed food, played English games and learned
how wise the Magna Carta was, how hard the Hanoverians

had tried, the measure and complexity of verse,
the hum and score of the whole orchestra.
At three o'clock I caught two buses home

where sometimes in the late afternoon
at a piano pushed into a corner of the playroom
my father would sit down and play the slow

lilts of Tom Moore while I stood there trying
not to weep at the cigarette smoke stinging up
from between his fingers and—as much as I could think—

I thought this is my country, was, will be again,
this upward-straining song made to be
our safe inventory of pain. And I was wrong.

THE WILD SPRAY

It came to me one afternoon in summer—
a gift of long-stemmed flowers in a wet
contemporary sheath of newspapers
which pieced off easily at the sink.

I put them in an ironstone jug
near the window; now years later
I know the names for the flowers
they were, but not the shape they made:

the true rose beside the mountain rose,
the muslin finery of asparagus fern,
rosemary, forsythia; something about it was
confined and free in the days that followed

which were the brute, final days of summer—
a consistency of milk about the heat haze,
midges freighting the clear space between
the privet and the hedge, the nights chilling

quickly into stars, the morning breaking late
and on the low table the wild spray
lasted for days, a sweet persuasion,
a random guess becoming a definition.

I have remembered it in a certain way—
displaced yellows and the fluencies
of colors in a jug making a statement of
the unfurnished grace of white surfaces,

the way I remember us when we first came here
and had no curtains; the lights on the mountain

that winter were sharp, distant promises
like crocuses through the snowfall of darkness.

We stood together at an upstairs window
enchanted by the patterns in the haphazard,
watching the street lamp making rain into
a planet of tears near the whitebeam trees.

NOCTURNE

After a friend has gone I like the feel of it:
The house at night. Everyone asleep.
The way it draws in like atmosphere or evening.

One o'clock. A floral teapot and a raisin scone.
A tray waits to be taken down.
The landing light is off. The clock strikes. The cat

comes into his own, mysterious on the stairs,
a black ambivalence around the legs of button-back
chairs, an insinuation to be set beside

the red spoon and the salt-glazed cup,
the saucer with the thick spill of tea
which scalds off easily under the tap. Time

is a tick, a purr, a drop. The spider
on the dining room window has fallen asleep
among complexities as I will once

the doors are bolted and the keys tested
and the switch turned up of the kitchen light
which made outside in the back garden

an electric room—a domestication
of closed daisies, an architecture
instant and improbable.

LISTEN. THIS IS THE
NOISE OF MYTH

This is the story of a man and woman
under a willow and beside a weir
near a river in a wooded clearing.
They are fugitives. Intimates of myth.

Fictions of my purpose. I suppose
I shouldn't say that yet or at least
before I break their hearts or save their lives
I ought to tell their story and I will:

when they went first it was winter; cold,
cold through the Midlands and as far west
as they could go. They knew they had to go—
through Meath, Westmeath, Longford,

their lives unraveling like the hours of light
and then there were lambs under the snow
and it was January, aconite and jasmine
and the hazel yellowing and puce berries on the ivy.

They could not eat where they had cooked
nor sleep where they had eaten
nor at dawn rest where they had slept.
They shunned the densities

of trees with one trunk and of caves
with one dark and the dangerous embrace
of islands with a single landing place.
And all the time it was cold, cold:

the fields still gardened by their ice,
the trees stitched with snow overnight,

the ditches full; frost toughening lichen,
darning lace into rock crevices.

And then the woods flooded and buds
blunted from the chestnut and the foxglove
put its big leaves out and chaffinches
chinked and flirted in the branches of the ash.

And here we are where we started from—
under a willow and beside a weir
near a river in a wooded clearing.
The woman and the man have come to rest.

Look how light is coming through the ash.
The weir sluices kingfisher blues.
The woman and the willow tree lean forward, forward.
Something is near; something is about to happen;

something more than spring
and less than history. Will we see
hungers eased after months of hiding?
Is there a touch of heat in that light?

If they stay here soon it will be summer; things
returning, sunlight fingering minnowy deeps,
seedy greens, reeds, electing lights
and edges from the river. Consider

legend, self-deception, sin, the sum
of human purpose and its end; remember
how our poetry depends on distance,
aspect: gravity will bend starlight.

Forgive me if I set the truth to rights.
Bear with me if I put an end to this:

She never turned to him; she never leaned
under the sallow-willow over to him.

They never made love; not there; not here;
not anywhere; there was no winter journey;
no aconite, no birdsong and no jasmine,
no woodland and no river and no weir.

Listen. This is the noise of myth. It makes
the same sound as shadow. Can you hear it?
Daylight grays in the preceptories.
Her head begins to shine

pivoting the planets of a harsh nativity.
They were never mine. This is mine:
This sequence of evicted possibilities.
Displaced facts. Tricks of light. Reflections.

Invention. Legend. Myth. What you will.
The shifts and fluencies are infinite.
The moving parts are marvelous. Consider
how the bereavements of the definite

are easily lifted from our heroine.
She may or she may not. She was or wasn't
by the water at his side as dark
waited above the western countryside.

O consolations of the craft.
How we put
the old poultices on the old sores,
the same mirrors to the old magic. Look.

The scene returns. The willow sees itself
drowning in the weir and the woman

gives the kiss of myth her human heat.
Reflections. Reflections. He becomes her lover.

The old romances make no bones about it.
The long and short of it. The end and the beginning.
The glories and the ornaments are muted.
And when the story ends the song is over.

II

Domestic
Interior

DEGAS'S LAUNDRESSES

You rise, you dawn
roll-sleeved Aphrodites,
out of a camisole brine,
a linen pit of stitches,
silking the fitted sheets
away from you like waves.

You seam dreams in the folds
of wash from which freshes
the whiff and reach of fields
where it bleached and stiffened.
Your chat's sabbatical:
brides, wedding outfits,

a pleasure of leisured women
are sweated into the folds,
the neat heaps of linen.
Now the drag of the clasp.
Your wrists basket your waist.
You round to the square weight.

Wait. There. Behind you.
A man. There behind you.
Whatever you do don't turn.
Why is he watching you?
Whatever you do don't turn.
Whatever you do don't turn.

See he takes his ease,
staking his easel so,
slowly sharpening charcoal,

closing his eyes just so,
slowly smiling as if
so slowly he is

unbandaging his mind.
Surely a good laundress
would understand its twists,
its white turns,
its blind designs:

it's your winding sheet.

Breakfast over, islanded by noise,
she watches the machines go fast and slow.
She stands among them as they shake the house.
They move. Their destination is specific.
She has nowhere definite to go.
She might be a pedestrian in traffic.

indefinite feeling ?

White surfaces retract. White
sideboards light the white of walls.
Cups wink white in their saucers.
The light of day bleaches as it falls
on cups and sideboards. She could use
the room to tap with if she lost her sight.

purity

give shape t

Machines jigsaw everything she knows.
And she is everywhere among their furor:
the tropic of the dryer tumbling clothes.
The round lunar window of the washer.
The kettle in the toaster is a kingfisher
swooping for trout above the river's mirror.

The wash done, the kettle boiled, the sheets
spun and clean, the dryer stops dead.
The silence is a death. It starts to bury
the room in white spaces. She turns to spread
a cloth on the board and irons sheets
in a room white and quiet as a mortuary.

A BALLAD OF
BEAUTY AND TIME

Plainly came the time
the eucalyptus tree
could not succour me,
nor the honey pot,
the sunshine vitamin.
Not even getting thin.
I had passed my prime.

Then, when bagged ash,
scalded quarts of water,
oil of the lime,
cinders for the skin
and honey all had failed,
I sorted out my money
and went to buy some time.

I knew the right address:
the occult house of shame
where all the women came
shopping for a mouth,
a new nose, an eyebrow
and entered without knocking
and stood as I did now.

A shape with a knife
stooped away from me
cutting something vague—
I couldn't really see—
it might have been a face.
I coughed once and said
—I want a lease of life.

The room was full of masks:
lines of grins gaping,
a wall of skin stretching,
a chin he had reworked,
a face he had remade.
He slit and tucked and cut,
then straightened from his blade.

"A tuck, a hem" he said—
"I only seam the line.
I only mend the dress.
It wouldn't do for you:
your quarrel's with the weave.
The best I achieve
is just a stitch in time."

I started out again.
I knew a studio
strewn with cold heels,
closed in marble shock.
I saw the sculptor there
chiseling a nose,
and buttonholed his smock:

"It's all very well
when you have bronzed a woman—
pinioned her and finned
wings on either shoulder.
Anyone can see
she won't get any older.
What good is that to me?

"See the last of youth
slumming in my skin,
my sham pink mouth.
Here behold your critic—
the threat to your aesthetic.

I am the brute proof:
beauty is not truth."

"Truth is in our lies—"
he angrily replied.
"This woman, fledged in stone,
the center of all eyes,
her own museum blind:
we sharpen with our skills
the arts of compromise.

"And all I have cast
in crystal or in glass,
in lapis or in onyx,
comes from my knowledge when—
above the honest flaw—
to lift and stay my hand
and say 'let it stand.' "

THE SERPENT
IN THE GARDEN

How often
in this loneliness,
unlighted
but for the porcelain

brightening
of the bath,
have I done this.
Again and again this.

This time,
in the shadowy
and woody light
between the bath and blind,

between the day and night,
the same blue
eyeshadow
rouge and blusher

will mesh with
my fingers
to a weaving
pulse.

In a ringed
coiling,
a convulsion,
I will heave

to a sinuous
and final
shining off
of skin:

look at the hood
I have made
for my eyes,
my head

and how quickly,
over my lips,
slicked and cold,
my tongue flickers.

POSE

After the painting *Mrs. Bedham* by Ingres

She is a housekeeping, a spring-cleaning.

A swept, tidied, emptied, kept woman.

Her rimmed hat, its unkempt streamers,
neaten to the seams of a collar
frilled and pat as a dressing table,
its pressed lace and ruching hardly able
to hide the solid column of her neck.

Reckless fashion masking common sense!

She smirks uneasily at what she's shirking,
sitting on this chair in silly clothes,
posing in a truancy of frills.

There's no repose in these broad knees,
The shawl she wears just upholsters her.

She hands the open book like pantry keys.

"DAPHNE WITH HER THIGHS IN BARK"

[Ezra Pound]

so that,
in the next myth,
my sister will be wiser.

Let her learn from me:

the opposite of passion
is not virtue
but routine.

Look at me.
I can be cooking,
making coffee,
scrubbing wood, perhaps,
and back it comes:
the crystalline, the otherwhere,
the wood

where I was
when he began the chase.
And how I ran from him!

Pan-thighed,
satyr-faced he was.

The trees reached out to me,
I silvered and
I quivered. I shook out my foil of quick leaves.

He snouted past.
What a fool I was!

I shall be here forever,
setting out the tea,
among the coppers and the branching alloys and
the tin shine of this kitchen;
laying saucers on the pine table.

Save face, sister.
Fall. Stumble.
Rut with him.
His rough heat will keep you warm.

You will be better off than me,
with your memories,
down the garden
at the start of March—

unable to keep your eyes
off the chestnut tree:

just the way
it thrusts and hardens.

THE NEW PASTORAL

The first man had flint to spark. He had a wheel
to read his world.

I'm in the dark.

I am a lost, last inhabitant—
displaced person in a pastoral chaos.

All day I listen to the loud distress, the switch
and tick of new herds.

But I'm no shepherdess.

Can I unbruise these sprouts or cleanse this mud flesh
till it roots again?
Can I make whole
this lamb's knuckle, butchered from its last crooked suckling?

I could be happy here,
I could be something more than a refugee

were it not for this lamb unsuckled, for the nonstop
switch and tick
telling me

there was a past, there was a pastoral,
and these chance sights—
what are they but amnesias of a rite

I danced once on a frieze?

THE WOMAN TURNS
HERSELF INTO A FISH

Unpod
the bag,
the seed.

Slap
the flanks back.
Flatten

paps.
Make finny,
scaled

and chill
the slack
and dimple

of the rump.
Pout
the mouth,

brow the eyes
and now
and now

eclipse
in these hips,
these loins,

the moon,
the blood
flux.

It's done.
I turn.
I flab upward.

blub-lipped,
hipless,
and I am

sexless,
shed
of ecstasy,

a pale
swimmer
sequin-skinned,

pearling eggs
screamlessly
in seaweed.

It's what
I set my heart on.
Yet,

ruddering
and muscling
in the sunless tons

of new freedoms,
still
I feel

a chill pull,
a brightening,
a light, a light:

and how
in my loomy cold,
my greens

still
she moons
in me.

THE MUSE MOTHER

My window pearls wet.
The bare rowan tree
berries rain.

I can see
from where I stand
a woman hunkering—
her busy hand
worrying a child's face,

working a nappy liner
over his sticky, loud
round of a mouth.

Her hand's a cloud
across his face,
making light and rain,
smiles and a frown,
a smile again.

She jockeys him to her hip,
pockets the nappy liner,
collars rain on her nape
and moves away,

but my mind stays fixed:

If I could only decline her—
lost noun
out of context,
stray figure of speech—
from this rainy street

again to her roots,
she might teach me
a new language:

to be a sibyl,
able to sing the past
in pure syllables,
limning hymns sung
to belly wheat or a woman

able to speak at last
my mother tongue.

IN THE GARDEN

Let's go out now
before the morning
gets warm.
Get your bicycle,

your teddy bear—
the one that's penny-colored
like your hair—
and come.

I want to show you
what
I don't exactly know.
We'll find out.

It's our turn
in this garden,
by this light,
among the snails

and daisies—
one so slow
and one so closed—
to learn.

I could show you things:
how the poplar root
is pushing through,
how your apple tree is doing,

how daisies
shut like traps.
But you're happy
as it is

and innocence
that until this
was just
an abstract water,

welling elsewhere
to refresh,
is risen here
my daughter:

before the dew,
before the bloom
the snail was here.
The whole morning is his loom

and this is truth,
this is brute grace
as only instinct knows
how to live it:

turn to me
your little face.
It shows a trace still,
an inkling of it.

ON RENOIR'S
THE GRAPE-PICKERS

They seem to be what they are harvesting:

rumps, elbows, hips, clustering
plumply in the sun; a fuss of shines
wining from the ovals of their elbows.

Flesh and shadow mesh inside each other.
Such roundness, such a sound vintage
of circles, such a work of pure spheres!
The brush plucks them from a tied vine.

But not this one: this redheaded woman.
Her skirt's a wave gathered to the weather.
Her eyes are closed; her hands are loosening.
Her ears are fisted in a dozed listening.
She dreams of stoves, raked leaves and plums.

When she wakes summer will be over.

DOMESTIC INTERIOR

1 Night Feed

This is dawn.
Believe me
This is your season, little daughter.
The moment daisies open,
The hour mercurial rainwater
Makes a mirror for sparrows.
It's time we drowned our sorrows.

I tiptoe in.
I lift you up
Wriggling
In your rosy, zipped sleeper.
Yes, this is the hour
For the early bird and me
When finder is keeper.

I crook the bottle.
How you suckle!
This is the best I can be,
Housewife
To this nursery
Where you hold on,
Dear Life.

A silt of milk.
The last suck.
And now your eyes are open,
Birth-colored and offended.
Earth wakes.
You go back to sleep.
The feed is ended.

Worms turn.
Stars go in.
Even the moon is losing face.
Poplars stilt for dawn
And we begin
The long fall from grace.
I tuck you in.

2 Monotony

The stilled hub
and polar drab
of the suburb
closes in.

In the round
of the staircase,
my arms sheafing nappies,
I grow in and down

to an old spiral,
a well of questions,
an oracle:
will it tell me—

am I
at these altars,
warm shrines—
washing machines, dryers

with their incense
of men and infants—
priestess
or sacrifice?

My later tasks
wait like children:
milk bottles,
the milkman's note.

Cold air
clouds the rinsed,
milky glass,
blowing clear

with a hint
of winter constellations:
will I find
my answer where

Virgo reaps?
Her arms sheafing
the hemisphere,
hour after frigid hour,

her virgin stars,
her maidenhead
married to force,
harry us

to wed our gleams
to brute routines:
solstices,
small families

3 Energies

This is my time:
the twilight closing in,
a hissing on the ring,
stove noises, kettle steam
and children's kisses.

But the energy of flowers—
their faces are so white,
my garden daisies,
they are so tight-fisted—
such economies of light!

In the dusk they have made hay:
in a banked radiance,
in an acreage of brightness
they are misering the day,
while mine delays away

in things left to do:
the soup, the bath, the fire.
Then bedtime.
Up the stairs.
And there, there

the buttery curls,
the light,
the bran fur of the teddy bear.
The fist like a nighttime daisy:
damp and tight.

4 H y m n

Four a.m.
December.
A lamb would perish
out there.

The cutlery glitter
of that sky
has nothing in it
I want to follow.

Here is the star
of my nativity:
the nursery lamp
in that suburb window,

behind which
is boiled glass, a bottle,
and a baby all
hisses like a kettle.

The light goes out.
The blackbird
takes up his part.
I wake by habit.
I have it off by heart:

these candles,
and the altar
and the psaltery of dawn.

And in the dark
as we slept
the world
was made flesh.

5 Patchwork

I have been thinking at random
on the universe,
or rather, how nothing in the universe
is random—

(there's nothing like presumption late at night.)

My sumptuous
trash bag of colors
Laura Ashley cottons—
waits to be cut
and stitched and patched but

there's a mechanical feel
about the handle
of my secondhand sewing machine,
with its flowers,
and "Singer" painted orange
and its iron wheel.

My back is to the dark.
Somewhere out there
are stars and bits of stars
and little bits of bits,
and swiftnesses and brightnesses and drift—
but is it craft or art?

I will be here
till midnight,
cross-legged in the dining room,
logging triangles and diamonds,
cutting and aligning,
finding greens in pinks
and burgundies in whites,
until I finish it.

There's no reason in it.

Only when it's laid
right across the floor—
sphere on square
and seam to seam
in a good light—
will it start to hit me:

these are not bits
they are pieces
and the pieces fit.

6 Endings

A child
shifts in a cot.
No matter what happens now
I won't fill one again.

It's a night
white things ember in:
jasmine and the shine—
flowering, opaline—
of the apple trees.

If I lean
I can see
what it is the branches end in:

The leaf.
The reach.
The blossom. The abandon.

7 Fruit on a Straight-Sided Tray

When the painter takes the straight-sided tray
and arranges late melons with grapes and lemons,
the true subject is the space between them:

in which repose the pleasure of these ovals
is seen to be an assembly of possibilities;
a deliberate collection of cross-purposes:

gross blues and purples, yellow and the shadow of bloom.
The room smells of metal polish. The afternoon sun
brings light but not heat; and no distraction from

the study of absences, the science of relationships
in which the abstraction is made actual: such as
fruit on a straight-sided tray; a homely arrangement.

This is the geometry of the visible, physical tryst
between substances, disguising for a while the equation
that kills: you are my child and between us are

spaces, distances. Growing to infinities.

8 After a Childhood
away from Ireland

One summer
we slipped in at dawn,
on plum-colored water
in the sloppy quiet.

The engines
of the ship stopped.
There was an eerie
drawing near,

a noiseless coming head-on
of red roofs, walls,
dogs, barley stooks.
Then we were there.

Cobh.
Coming home.
I had heard of this:
the ground the emigrants

resistless, weeping,
laid their cheeks to,
put their lips to kiss.
Love is also memory.

I only stared.
What I had lost
was not land
but the habit of land:

whether of growing out of,
or settling back on,

or being
defined by.

I climb
to your nursery.
I stand listening
to the dissonances

of the summer's day endii
I bend to kiss you.
Your cheeks
are brick pink.

9 Domestic Interior

FOR KEVIN

The woman is as round
as the new ring
ambering her finger.
The mirror weds her.
She has long since been bedded.

There is
about it all
a quiet search for attention,
like the unexpected shine
of a despised utensil.

The oils,
the varnishes,
the cracked light,
the worm of permanence—
all of them supplied by Van Eyck—

by whose edict she will stay
burnished, fertile
on her wedding day,
interred in her joy.
Love, turn.

The convex of your eye
that is so loving, bright
and constant yet shows
only this woman in her varnishes,
who won't improve in the light.

But there's a way of life
that is its own witness:
put the kettle on, shut the blind.

Home is a sleeping child,
an open mind

and our effects,
shrugged and settled
in the sort of light
jugs and kettles
grow important by.